ICE AGE SETTLEMENT

Between 300,000 and 100,000 years ago, a species of humans known as Neanderthals lived in Eurasia. Neanderthals were named after the Neander Valley in Germany where their remains were first discovered.

They lived during an ice age and many sheltered in caves and rocky outcrops. This is why they are often referred to as 'cave men'. Despite their primitive existence, scientists believe that Neanderthals were actually quite intelligent.

WOOLLY MAMMOTHS

Woolly mammoths were hunted by Neanderthals. These animals could provide plenty of food and their hides could be used for clothing. Mammoths had a very thick layer of hair, so their coats were used to keep people warm in the cold climate.

Mammoths were similar in size to African elephants. They could measure four metres in height and weigh 6,000 kilograms.

EXTINCTION

Woolly mammoths all but died out approximately 10,000 years ago. A small population, however, of no more than 1,000 woolly mammoths, lived on an island in Russia (Wrangel Island) until 4,300 years ago.

SHELTER

A 44,000-year-old shelter was discovered in 2011. It was built from mammoth bones.

Some scientists believe that Neanderthals formed their own language and were capable of speaking to one another.

Neanderthals were powerfully built and had bigger brains than us. They made stone tools and used spears made of wood to hunt.

FIRE

Neanderthals domesticated fire and used it to keep warm and to deter predators.

Neanderthals died out roughly 30,000–40,000 years ago.

ABORIGINAL SETTLEMENT

The Aboriginal people journeyed from areas of Southeast Asia to Australia by walking across land that has long since been submerged by rising sea levels. Evidence suggests that they reached Australian shores in 45,000 BCE (though it may have been several thousand years earlier) and spread across the colossal island, creating settlements along the way.

RAINBOW SERPENT

In Aboriginal lore, the Rainbow Serpent could generate storms, floods and rivers. The snake had life-giving powers and helped create humankind. Some cave paintings of the Rainbow Serpent can be traced as far back as 6,000–8,000 years.

DIDGERIDOO

This musical instrument was invented by the Aboriginal people. Carved from tree trunks, some experts think that it may even be the oldest musical instrument in history.

ULURU

Uluru, also known as Ayers Rock, is the largest monolith (single piece of rock) on Earth. It is considered sacred by the Australian Aboriginals.

The Aboriginals created unique artworks on rock formations and cave walls, depicting animals, deities and patterns.

BOOMERANGS

Aboriginals used boomerangs to hunt. They could be thrown to immobilize creatures in the air and on land.

DREAMTIME

Dreamtime or the Dreaming is an integral part of Aboriginal spirituality and religious lore. Dreamtime refers to the period in the distant past when the planet's environments and geological formations were fabricated and human life was created.

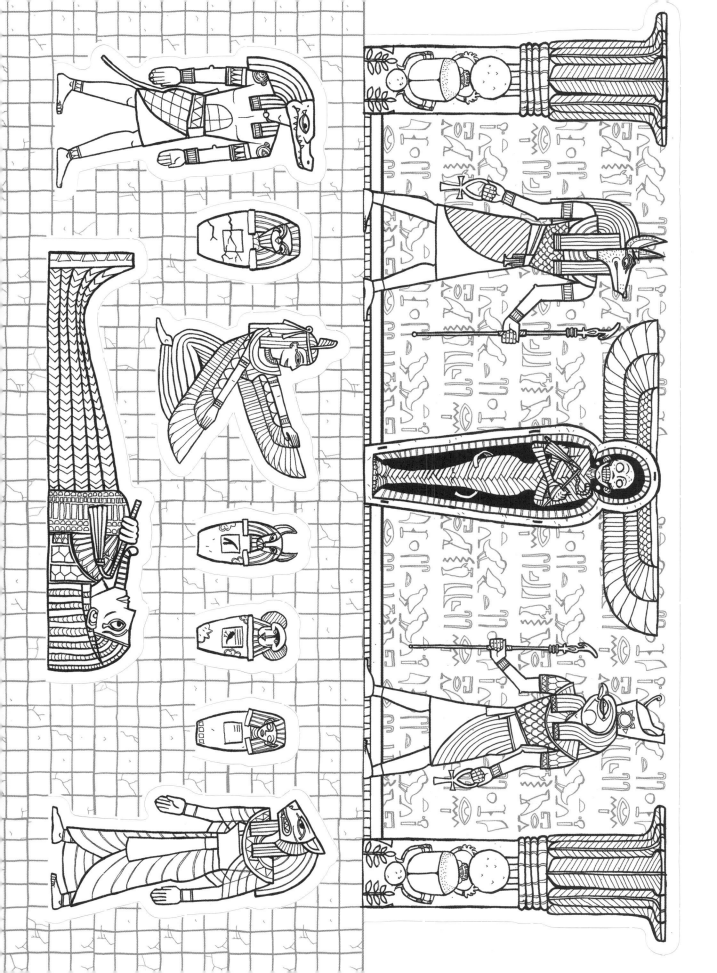

ANCIENT EGYPTIAN TOMB

The ancient Egyptians believed in more than 1,500 gods and built impressive tombs and temples to honour them. Each deity had different functions and roles and some were depicted with animal heads to convey their characteristics.

The people believed that life continued after death, so they preserved dead bodies by turning them into mummies. They popped a corpse's lungs, liver, stomach and intestines into canopic jars, dried the body with a special salt called natron, and then wrapped it from head to toe in bandages. This process took up to 70 days to complete. Afterwards, the mummy was placed in a coffin and buried with all sorts of important possessions to take along to the afterlife. Some pharaohs even had their slaves and pets entombed with them.

TEFNUT
The goddess of rain and moisture

Tefnut was created from the spit of her father, Ra (the sun god).

CANOPIC JARS

MA'AT
The goddess of truth, justice, harmony and balance

Ma'at decided whether or not a deceased person would reach the afterlife by weighing their soul.

SARCOPHAGUS

Pharaohs were buried in ornate coffins known as sarcophagi. The most famous sarcophagus belonged to a pharaoh called Tutankhamun. The Egyptians adorned his casket with more than 110 kilograms of pure gold.

SOBEK
The god of waterways

Sobek was a protector of Egyptian people. He also enjoyed eating flesh. Live crocodiles were kept in pools at temples to honour him.

THE CITY OF BABYLON

Babylon's foundations were built roughly 4,000 years ago. It was ruled by several different tribes during its existence and was even destroyed in 689 BCE by a people called the Assyrians.

Babylon was rebuilt in the 7th and 6th centuries BCE. Under the rule of King Nebuchadnezzar II, it became the largest city in the world.

The city prospered until 539 BCE, when it was attacked by the Persian army. The Babylonians were captured, sparking an end to their way of life.

ETEMENANKI

Etemenanki was a temple built to honour the god Marduk. It was an enormous example of a style of building known as a ziggurat – a tiered pyramid.

WINGED STATUES (LAMASSU)

Statues of winged bulls and lions appear in many different cultures, especially in the Middle East. The Babylonians built the statues to protect doorways and gates from evil intruders.

THE HANGING GARDENS

According to ancient writings, King Nebuchadnezzar II built the Hanging Gardens in honour of his wife, Amytis of Media, who longed to see the lush trees and plants that grew in her homeland. The gardens were one of Seven Ancient Wonders of the World.

MARDUK

The god of thunderstorms

The Babylonian people praised Marduk above all of the other gods. He eventually became Lord of the Gods of Heaven and Earth after defeating Tiamat in combat.

TIAMAT

The goddess of the sea and a symbol of chaos

Tiamat formed an allegiance with Apsu (the god of freshwater), and gave birth to other gods. When Apsu was killed, Tiamat gave birth to dragons to avenge his death.

THE ACROPOLIS

The Acropolis in the Greek city of Athens was a hub of religious and political activity. It is often called the birthplace of democracy (which means 'rule by the people'). Democracy gave the Athenian people the right to discuss and vote for new laws and to govern their own affairs. Only free men could vote – women, slaves, children and outsiders were not allowed.

ZEUS

The Greeks believed that Zeus (the king of the gods) could launch lightning bolts.

ATHENA PROMACHOS

This enormous bronze statue was more than 9 metres tall.

THE PARTHENON

This enormous temple was built in the 5th century BCE to honour Athena, the ancient Greek goddess of war, handicraft and practical reason. It can still be seen today.

OLYMPIANS

The Greeks believed in 12 major gods, known as the Olympians: Aphrodite, Apollo, Ares, Artemis, Athena, Demeter, Dionysus, Hades, Hera, Hermes, Poseidon and Zeus.

CHARIOT

Chariot racing in ancient Greece was a dangerous spectacle. Riders and horses were often injured in the races.

SOCRATES

Socrates, one of history's most famous philosophers, lived in Athens.

GREEK SOLDIER

The Greek army was a formidable force. The most fearsome warriors were from a state called Sparta. Spartan soldiers began their training at the age of seven.

GRECIAN URNS

Many Grecian pots, urns and vases were decorated with ornate patterns, characters, myths and stories.

TERRACOTTA ARMY

Before he died in 210 BCE, Shihuangdi, the first Chinese Emperor, decided to create a stupendous tomb. He employed approximately 700,000 workers to adorn his burial chamber. They handcrafted more than 8,000 soldiers, horses and chariots to decorate the crypt. It took them over 30 agonizing years to complete the work.

Shihuangdi spent his life trying to find the secret to immortality.

No two soldiers are the same and all were made by hand.

DISCOVERING THE TOMB

More than 2,100 years after the tomb was built, farmers discovered the site by accident while trying to dig a well.

The tomb is rumoured to contain a miniature model of the whole empire, complete with rivers made of mercury (quicksilver) and contraptions to control the tides.

Excavators have to be extremely careful with the fragile, life-sized figures.

HORSES

More than 650 terracotta horses have been discovered at the site.

Shihuangdi's burial chamber is yet to be excavated. It is thought that it could be booby-trapped!

GLADIATORIAL ARENA

The ancient Romans were a bloodthirsty bunch. People would flock to gladiatorial arenas to watch men (and sometimes animals) fight to the death.

The largest arena, the Colosseum in Rome, could house more than 50,000 people. Known as an amphitheatre, meaning 'theatre with seats on all sides', it was built almost 2,000 years ago to host different types of performances, including plays, executions and gladiatorial battles. Some historians even think the arena could be flooded with water to re-enact famous naval battles.

SPARTACUS

The most famous gladiator was called Spartacus. He became the leader of more than 100,000 slaves. Spartacus helped them fight against the Roman army in southern Italy.

Spartacus was eventually killed by the Romans. His rebellion helped empower the slaves, and leaders were more cautious in their treatment of them after this.

LION

Beasts and exotic creatures were brought to the arenas from all corners of the Roman Empire. During particularly bloodthirsty games, thousands of animals were killed in just one day!

GLADIATOR

These fearsome warriors were trained in the art of combat. Before they became gladiators, most were slaves or criminals.

GALLIC HELMET

GLADIUS

Gladius was the Latin word for the short sword used by ancient Roman foot soldiers.

VIKING LONGBOAT

The Vikings came from Denmark, Norway and Sweden. For more than three centuries, Viking warriors travelled across Europe, raiding settlements and trading with locals. Some traders even made it as far as Iraq in the east and North America in the west.

KRAKEN

Often depicted with giant tentacles and a tremendous appetite for human flesh, the Kraken appears in Norse mythology. It was said to dwell off the coast of Norway.

VIKING LONGBOAT

Built from oak, these ships were approximately 20 metres long. Longboats could navigate knee-deep waters and shores thanks to their streamlined shape and shallow hull. This meant Vikings could attack coastal villages with extreme speed.

When Viking warriors died, they were sometimes buried on their longboats, along with many of their possessions. People believed that the ships would travel to Valhalla, home of Odin (the god of war and death). In Valhalla, dead warriors could fight all day long and feast all night.

VALKYRIES

In myth, Valkyries were female figures who decided which warriors lived and died in battle. They also looked after the warriors in Valhalla.

Around 500 years before Christoper Columbus travelled to the Americas, the Vikings landed in what is now called Canada. The unfortunate travellers were attacked by a tribe of natives, however, and forced to flee.

MEDIEVAL JOUST

Jousting was a popular, but extremely dangerous, medieval sport. To win, a knight had to unsaddle the other rider using a long and cumbersome weapon known as a lance. Lances were made from solid wood and were incredibly heavy.

Jousts took place at European tournaments and feasts during the Middle Ages (5th–15th century CE). As well as honour and fame, the winner of a tournament often won a purse full of coins or his opponent's horse and armour.

SHIELD

Shields were used for protection and were often decorated with a coat of arms.

ARMOUR

Knights wore plenty of armour to protect themselves. Some coats of armour could weigh as much as 25 kilograms.

BROADSWORD

The broadsword, a popular weapon during medieval times, was double-edged. It was used to cut and slice, rather than stab.

CHIVALRY

Knights obeyed a strict code of honour, courage and morality, known as chivalry.

The process of becoming a knight was not easy or swift. First, a boy had to be of noble (aristocratic) birth. Aged seven, he worked as a page, learning how to fight and ride horses. After several years he could become a squire, working directly for a knight and assisting him in his daily duties. When a squire had proven himself, he was knighted by a nobleman or by the king himself.

MORNING STAR

This weapon had a spiky weight at one end to inflict injury.

SAMURAI WARRIORS

The samurai were an elite class of Japanese warriors. They helped govern Japan from the 12th–19th century CE. Samurai were originally part of the Japanese aristocracy. The soldiers were known as *bushi* and they helped protect the country from rebels and foreign invaders.

By the end of the 15th century, however, the samurai were at war with one another. A series of civil wars rocked the country, but somehow the samurai managed to keep their unique way of life intact. This all changed when the samurai successfully helped Emperor Meiji unify the country in 1868. Trade routes opened up with the USA, giving Japan access to industrial technology, and the Emperor no longer had a real need for the samurai army. Many samurai were forced to find ordinary jobs due to poverty. In 1876, the Emperor made it illegal for samurai to wear their swords – this signified the end of their dynasty.

The samurai weren't just well-versed in the art of combat, they were also trained in disciplines such as flower arranging and tea brewing.

Many women also fought alongside samurai in battle and protected lands and villages from invasion.

ARMOUR

Created from lots of metal and leather plates sewn together, samurai armour was extremely strong and much more flexible than European armour of the time.

A samurai's *kabuto* (helmet) was often ornate in its design. Many were decorated with horns and carvings. Some even had masks, known as *mempo*, to protect the wearer's face.

BUSHIDO

The samurai way of life was known as *bushido*. Like chivalry in medieval Europe, *bushido* focussed on combat, bravery, loyalty and honour.

GUNSEN

Japanese war fan

KATANA

A type of curved sword called a *katana* was used by samurai. These blades were famed for their sharpness.

A *katana* sword could cut through flesh and bone with ease and was made from steel so strong that it was difficult to blunt.

THE BLACK DEATH

The Black Death, also known as the bubonic plague, scourged Asia and Europe during the mid-1300s. The disease spread swiftly from country to country as ships carrying infected members of crew and flea-ridden rodents sailed the Mediterranean Sea, stopping at various ports. From 1347–1351, the Black Death killed approximately one-third of the European population, making it one of the most devastating diseases ever to affect humankind.

Many people fled to areas of countryside to evade the plague.

CROSSES

The cross symbol was used to mark the doors of infected homes.

CART

Horse-drawn carts were used to transport the dead away from cities, towns and villages.

BUBOES

The Black Death took its name from the colour of the swollen areas on plague victims.

POMANDER

Some wealthy folk carried small orbs (known as pomanders) filled with perfumes, herbs and infusions. These were sniffed to distract people from the noxious odours that filled medieval streets.

DOCTOR

It was almost impossible for doctors of the time to treat the disease. They wore bird-like masks to protect themselves from infection.

It is now widely accepted that the bloodsucking fleas on rodents carried the plague bacterium.

RAT

AZTEC CITY OF TENOCHTITLÁN

Tenochtitlán was a bustling city. At its busiest, it was home to approximately 400,000 people. The city was situated on islands in Lake Texcoco, Mexico, and was the capital of the Aztec Empire. Its location gave its inhabitants access to water, allowing them to farm and thrive.

The Aztec Empire prospered for more than two centuries, but came under threat when a Spanish soldier called Hernán Cortés arrived on Mexican shores in 1519. He attacked the city with guns and cavalry in 1521 and conquered the Aztec people.

TEMPLE OF HUITZILOPOCHTLI

Huitzilopochtli was the Aztec god of the sun and war. Aztec priests fed him human hearts to keep him happy.

Tenochtitlán housed a huge palace belonging to an Aztec emperor called Montezuma II. The palace is rumoured to have had in excess of 300 rooms.

AZTEC CALENDAR

The Aztecs held many festivals for all of their gods. It was vital that they celebrate on the correct day, so they created calendars to keep track of time.

After Hernán Cortés sacked the city, many Aztecs died from new diseases that were brought over by European ships.

The Aztecs were a warmongering people. They conquered many of the surrounding tribes in Mexico, enslaving their prisoners and sacrificing many to the gods.

AZTEC WARRIORS

Some Aztec soldiers dressed up as animals. The most highly regarded were the eagle and jaguar warriors.

TOTEM POLE

Native American tribes used totem poles to mark burial grounds, to represent events and stories, and to honour their cultural beliefs.

NATIVE AMERICAN SETTLEMENT

Long before Europeans reached American shores, hundreds of Native American tribes were spread across the country. As more and more settlers flocked to America during the 19th century, competition for land became fierce. Many native tribes were pushed away from their territories by armed settlers and by the US government. Eventually, vicious battles for land erupted. The most famous skirmish was called 'Battle of the Little Bighorn'.

TIPI

These tents, made from animal skins, provided protection from wind, rain and intense sunlight.

Native Americans first settled on the American continent in approximately 12,000 BCE.

HEADDRESSES

The ornate headdresses of the Sioux could only be worn by warriors who had proven their bravery in battle. Some were made from eagle feathers and thought to be full of spiritual power. One of the most famous warriors was called Crazy Horse. He led his people to many victories in battle.

SITTING BULL

Sitting Bull was a famous member of the Sioux people. He helped lead them to a great military victory over General Custer (and the US army) at the Battle of the Little Bighorn in 1876.

KAYAK

Kayaks were built and used by Native American people.

THE BATTLE OF THE SOMME

In 1916, a four-month long battle took place in Somme, an area in northern France. In the first day of fighting alone, more than 20,000 people died.

GAS MASKS

Chemical weapons, including mustard and chlorine gases, were used by both sides during WWI. The gases could burn, blind and suffocate, so it was important that soldiers had access to masks that could protect them from the noxious fumes.

TANKS

Tanks were used for the first time in WWI. They could travel over muddy, uneven ground and protect their inhabitants from gunshots and shrapnel. As the technology was fairly new, though, many tanks broke down on the battlefields.

NO MAN'S LAND

The area between opposing trenches was known as No Man's Land. It was often riddled with barbed wire, bodies, puddles and craters.

WWI TRENCHES

The First World War began in 1914. It was fought between the Allies (most notably the British Empire, France and Russia) and the Central Powers (Austria–Hungary and Germany). As the war progressed, other countries joined the conflict (including Greece, Italy, Portugal and the United States for the Allies, and Bulgaria and the Ottoman Empire for the Central Powers). The majority of battles were fought in France and Belgium, where armies dug trenches in the ground to protect themselves. The war finished on 11th November, 1918. More than eight million soldiers died in battle and millions of civilians were caught up in the crossfire.

Soldiers in the trenches were constantly cold and wet during the winter months and often struggled with various ailments, including 'trench foot' (a grim infection of the skin on the feet).

APOLLO 11 MOON LANDING

On 20th July, 1969, humankind successfully managed to land on the Moon. The Apollo 11 space mission was conducted by the USA. It successfully transported three men to the Moon and back. Michael Collins stayed in the command module, while Neil Armstrong and Buzz Aldrin steered the lunar module to the Moon's surface.

Neil Armstrong and Buzz Aldrin spent almost 21 hours on the Moon's surface. Just over two of these hours were spent outside the lunar module.

The crew travelled a whopping 240,000 miles from the Earth to the Moon in just 76 hours.

APOLLO LUNAR MODULE

The Apollo lunar module (*Eagle*) transported Neil Armstrong and Buzz Aldrin from their command module (*Columbia*) to the Moon.

LUNAR LASER RANGING RETROREFLECTOR

This clever piece of kit was deployed to help scientists measure the distance between the Moon and Earth more accurately.

Approximately 600 million people watched the Moon landing on television.

THE SPACE RACE

The 'Space Race' was contested between the Soviet Union and the USA. Each country wanted to be the first to achieve new feats in space travel.

The Soviets were the first to send an astronaut into space. On 12th April, 1961, Yuri Gagarin completed one full orbit of Earth in his Vostok 1 spacecraft.

The Apollo space programme was not cheap. Its cost has been estimated at more than 25 billion dollars, which, in today's money, would be more than 100 billion dollars!

Astronauts Neil Armstrong and Buzz Aldrin were the first people to set foot on the Moon's surface.

The American flag they planted in the ground is still there to this day — though it is rumoured that the blast from the lunar module's thrusters knocked it over on take off.